# The F-117A
# Stealth Fighter

This reference is dedicated to both the pilots who flew the Have Blue experimental survivable testbed aircraft and to the pilots—past, present, and future—of the Senior Trend F-117A full-scale development and production aircraft. Thank you for just saluting and doing your job.

# The F-117A
# Stealth Fighter

Steve Pace

TAB AERO

Blue Ridge Summit, PA

FIRST EDITION
FIRST PRINTING

© 1992 by **TAB/AERO Books**, an imprint of TAB Books.
TAB Books is a division of McGraw-Hill, Inc.

**Library of Congress Cataloging-in-Publication Data**

Pace, Steve.
   The F-117A Stealth Fighter / by Steve Pace.
     p.    cm.
   Includes index.
   ISBN 0-8306-2795-2 (pbk.)
   1.  F117 (Jet fighter plane)  I. Title.
UG1242.F5P3   1992
358.4'383—dc20                91-34276
                             CIP

TAB Books offers software for sale. For information and a catalog, please contact
TAB Software Department, Blue Ridge Summit, PA 17294-0850.

Acquisitions Editor: Jeff Worsinger
Editor:  Steve Mesner
Director of Production: Katherine G. Brown
Book Design: Jaclyn J. Boone
Cover Design: Graphics Plus, Hanover, PA
Front and Back Cover Photographs courtesy of USAF.
   Photos by SMSGT Bob Wickley.               AS1

# Contents

# Acknowledgments

I gratefully appreciate the contributions of the following to this reference: Eric Schulzinger, Richard Stadler, Denny Lombard, April McKettrick, Lockheed; Richard Kennedy, Robert Salvucci, General Electric; Master Sgt. Bobby Shelton, 37th TFW Public Affairs; Dr. Ira Chart, Northrop; Tony Landis, Aviation Photographer; DOD Public Affairs; Bill Scott, *Aviation Week & Space Technology* magazine; and Senior Master Sgt. Bob Wickley, USAF Recruiting Service.

Thank you all very much indeed.

# Foreword

LOCKHEED'S F-117A Stealth Fighter, one of many exotic aircraft developed in the shadowy "Black World" of the company's Skunk Works, attracted attention well before its arrowhead-like faceted design was made public. It was unusual enough that people who saw or heard the quiet, strange-looking aircraft slip across the night sky hesitated to tell others. After all, people who reported "UFOs" usually had to endure nervous smiles and whispers from friends, family, and co-workers—and who needed that? But when the Air Force released a fuzzy photo of the F-117A in 1988, those same people could finally point and say, "That's what I saw!"

America's leap into the new world of low-observable or "stealthy" aircraft was not without problems. Two subscale "Have Blue" prototypes and the first production F-117A crashed. Some called it the "Wobblin' Goblin" in the early days, before flight control glitches were ironed out. Later, two of the operational fighters crashed, one close to Bakersfield, California. Only by keeping an airtight lid of security clamped on the development program were engineers and test pilots able to find and fix each problem. If the fighter had been built and tested in the unclassified "White World," nervous and overcritical politicians would have cancelled the program in a heartbeat.

The Air Force and Lockheed did a great job of keeping the program secret for about 10 years, allowing the aircraft to mature into a viable fighting machine. Problems were solved, and the United States went to war in early 1991 with a powerful new weapon system. While the world watched on TV, lone-wolf F-117As threaded the gantlet of missiles and tracers over downtown Baghdad to drop precision laser-guided bombs down elevator shafts only yards away from CNN's cameras.

Today, the F-117A routinely flies during daylight hours and appears at selected airshows. Still, taxpayers and airplane enthusiasts are kept at arm's length by no-nonsense armed guards. Even at the 1991 Paris Air Show, French dignitaries who simply tried to touch the fighter's black skin were told to keep their hands off. Lockheed and the Air Force are determined to keep many of the F-117A's secrets.

Thanks to persistent digging and rare interviews, Steve Pace has compiled a wealth of facts and history about every Stealth Fighter built to date. But he presents the Have Blue and F-117A stories in a way that preserves the swallow-tailed night attacker's mystique. And that's just as it should be. Until the veil of classification is lifted another notch or two, his book will be a vital reference for all who are fascinated by this, the first of a whole generation of military stealth aircraft.

BILL SCOTT

Senior Engineering Editor,
*Aviation Week & Space Technology*
Author, *Inside the Stealth Bomber:*
*The B-2 Story*

# Introduction

ON 10 NOVEMBER 1988, just 12 days before the rollout of the Northrop B-2 stealth bomber, the long-rumored existence of a stealth *fighter* was confirmed by the Pentagon during a media briefing. And, as assumed for nearly a decade, it was indeed a product of the Lockheed Corporation. Its official designation, often thought to be F-19A, was in fact F-117A. And its configuration, guessed to be rounded and smooth, was angular and jutted. Nevertheless, with the release of limited details and a single poor-quality photograph, the reality of a stealth fighter, the Lockheed F-117A, had been verified at last by the Department of Defense.

Designed, developed, and produced for the U.S. Air Force Tactical Air Command—under budget and ahead of schedule—by Lockheed Advanced Development Company—the "Skunk Works"—the F-117A is a dedicated user of low-observable, or stealth, technology. It is the first operational stealth fighter in the world. In fact, it is the first operational stealth air vehicle of any type anywhere in the world.

The unique design of the F-117A Black Jet (as its pilots and crewmembers prefer it to be called) provides exceptional combat capabilities. Approximately the size of a McDonnell Douglas F-15 Eagle, the semi-delta winged F-117A is powered by two non-augmented General Electric F404 turbofan engines and it incorporates a quadruple-redundant fly-by-wire flight control system to manage its inherently unstable flying characteristics. It has high subsonic speed, and, with aerial refueling, unlimited range.

Flown by the elite cadre of pilots of the U.S. Air Force Tactical Air Command's 37th Tactical Fighter Wing at Tonopah Test Range Airfield, Nevada, the single-place, twin-engine F-117A is optimized to penetrate dense threat environments and attack high-value targets with pinpoint accuracy. It supports worldwide commitments and enhances the deterrent strength of the U.S. armed forces.

The F-117A stealth fighter employs a variety of tactical ordnance and it is equipped with sophisticated navigation and attack systems. These are integrated into a state-of-the-art digital avionics suite that reduces pilot workload and aids mission effectiveness. Detailed planning for combat missions (sorties) into highly defended threat areas is accomplished by an automated mission planning system that was specifically developed to optimize the unique capabilities of the Black Jet.

The Lockheed F-117A is classified as a fighter/attack air vehicle but does not have the F/A prefix as used by the McDonnell Douglas F/A-18 Hornet. And since the designation F-19 has not been used, the designation F-117 came as a complete surprise to those "in the know"—especially since the designation F-111 was thought to be the last "Century Series" designator used before the Department of Defense began anew in 1962 with the designation F-1 and so on. Curiously, the designation gap between the F/A-18 Hornet and the F-20 Tigershark remains unexplained. And, by the way, what happened to the designations F-112 through F-116?

The F-117A Black Jet has proved that low-observable, or stealth, technology works.

It is capable of carrying and delivering in a precise manner both conventional and nuclear ordnance. Fully missionized, it is optimized to strike fixed and mobile targets, in all weather, and during nighttime.

One key to the survivability of the F-117A is its multifaceted exterior and overall configuration, which alone reduces its radar cross-section by as much as 85 percent. Its other signatures—heat and so on—are reduced by other means. And, counter to reports elsewhere, only about five percent of the F-117A's structure comprises composite materials.

The success of the F-117A program has demonstrated that a stealth fighter can be designed for reliability and maintainability. In reality, the maintenance statistics for the aircraft are comparable to other tactical fighters of similar size and complexity. Logistically supported by the Sacramento Air Logistics Center at McClellan Air Force Base, California, the F-117A is kept at the forefront of technology through a planned weapon system improvement program located at U.S. Air Force Plant 42, Palmdale, California.

Streamlined management by the U.S. Air Force Aeronautical Systems Division at Wright-Patterson Air Force Base, Ohio, combined breakthrough low-observable technology with concurrent developments (i.e., digital fly-by-wire flight control systems, composite materials, improved radar measurement processes, and so on) to rapidly field a first-generation stealth aircraft. The F-117A production decision was made in 1978 with a contract being awarded to the Lockheed Skunk Works. The first flight was made in 1981, just 31 months after the FSD (full-scale development) contract was received by Lockheed. The 37th Tactical Fighter Wing (formerly 4450th Tactical Group) achieved IOC (initial operational capability) in 1983, only 59 months after the FSD decision was made.

A total of 59 production F-117A stealth fighters have been procured. The first production airplane was delivered to and accepted by the Tactical Air Command in 1982; the last production airplane was delivered/accepted in 1990. No more than 8 aircraft were produced during any year. Total procurement cost for the F-117A program was $4.265 billion. This amount includes a flyaway cost of $2.514 billion for all aircraft, and a unit flyaway cost of $42.6 million for each F-117A airplane. The development cost of the aircraft was $1.9996 billion, and military construction (aircraft hangers, etc.) was $295.4 million. Total F-117A program cost was $6.5603 billion in "then year" monies (actual dollar amounts spent).

The F-117A stealth fighter does not have a "cloaking device" like the galactic battle cruisers in the *Star Trek* television series and movies; it is not invisible to the eye. It does, however, guard its most secret attributes from potential adversaries. And, without question, this is the way it should be. Yet those very same potential adversaries have witnessed the one deadly capability the F-117A does have: It strikes without detection. In other words, it does not have to be seen to fire. This was demonstrated during the recent air campaign against Iraq in Operation Desert Storm. Time and time again, F-117As delivered their precision-guided ordnance with pinpoint accuracy—and without a scratch.

The F-117A's success made it a superstar and fully displayed the value of stealth technology. The door to new stealth programs—especially stealth aircraft programs—is fully opened. It was the Lockheed F-117 Black Jet that led the way.

# 1

# Historical Overview

DEVELOPED AND PRODUCED for the U.S. Air Force Tactical Air Command (USAF/TAC) by Lockheed Advanced Development Company (LADC), better known as the "Skunk Works," the F-117A is the world's first operational fighter to use low-observable stealth technology for mission effectiveness and aircraft survivability. Flown by pilots of the 37th Tactical Fighter Wing—the Nighthawks—this single-seat, twin-engine fighter/attack airplane is optimized to deeply penetrate any dense threat environment at night and in weather and strike high-value targets with pinpoint accuracy. It relies on covert tactics for its survival.

## Covert Tactics

Covert tactics in military engagements are nothing new. The Trojan War, waged more than 3000 years ago, provides one example. In Greek legend, Greece made war against the city of Troy in 1193 B.C. to rescue Helen, wife of King Menelaus, who had been kidnapped by Paris, son of Priam of Troy. To accomplish her rescue, punish the Trojans, and decimate Troy (an ancient city in northwestern Asia Minor), the Greeks built a large hollow horse of wood, filled it with Greek soldiers, and left it outside the gates of Troy. Thinking the horse was a gift, the Trojans brought it into their heavily defended city. After nightfall, soldiers hidden inside the horse sneaked out and opened the sleeping city's gates. The Greek army, waiting outside, entered and destroyed Troy. The Trojan Horse, then, was used tactically in a covert way to win a military victory.

Many wars have been waged since the legendary Trojan War, and countless covert tactics have been used to defeat enemies—especially on the ground and at sea. But in the

*A Lockheed F-117A departs the main base area of Nellis AFB to return home to its Tonopah Test Range Airfield facility after coming home from Saudi Arabia. Bombing mission markings are notable.*

air, furtive tactics are relatively new. The primary covert tactic for manned air vehicles is low-observable stealth technology to make them less vulnerable and more survivable. Moreover, dedicated stealth aircraft have the ability to operate from secure areas, do their job without detection (until it is too late), then safely return to secure areas with minimal risk to their pilots. The recent success of the F-117A stealth fighter during Operation Desert Storm has confirmed the value of fully missionized covert, survivable, in-weather aircraft such as the Black Jet, the name F-117A pilots prefer to call their aircraft.

In the early 1970s, Russia developed and deployed new and advanced early warning radar networks, improved radar-guided SAMs (surface-to-air missiles), and better fighter/interceptor aircraft with look-down/shoot-down radar systems. These new and advanced systems presented a significant threat to conventional U.S. aircraft. This threat was demonstrated clearly during the last years of the Vietnam War, and once again in the Middle East War of 1973. Worse, the new threat could not be defeated by conventional electronic countermeasures (ECM) applications nor current military tactics. Therefore, a solution to Russia's growing threat had to be devised, developed, and implemented. It had to be an unconventional cure.

## Concurrent Technological Breakthroughs

Simultaneously, concurrent technological breakthroughs in low-observable (LO)—or "stealth"—technology for applications on aircraft were coming to the forefront. These included:

- Advanced composite materials for internal and external airframe and powerplant structures to reduce an aircraft's radar cross section (RCS).
- Improved radar-absorbing materials (RAM) and application processes of these special paint and putty materials to mask an aircraft's exterior protuberances such as rivets and gaps between panels and doors.
- Improved radar measurement devices to better reduce an aircraft's RCS—by as much as 85 percent—by way of external shaping alone.
- Advanced all-digital, fly-by-wire electronic flight control systems to replace basic aerodynamics lost to inherently unstable air vehicles about all three axes—pitch, roll, and yaw.
- Advanced computer-generated aircraft design processes to speed development time and reduce cost.
- Improved tactical weapons and advanced weapon delivery systems.

These discoveries, in part, made it possible to counter the Russian threat in an unconventional manner—specifically, with a stealth aircraft, the F-117A.

In late 1974, using the concurrent discoveries mentioned above, the Lockheed Skunk Works literally reinvented the airplane as mankind had known it. With a new design idea called *faceting*, whereby angular surfaces on an aircraft's exterior are employed to deflect radar beams (much as the light beam from a flashlight deflects off a flat surface), Lockheed engineers designed an LO airplane configuration that countered conventional aircraft design. With faceting, however, an obvious aerodynamic penalty surfaced: The airplane would be inherently unstable about all three axes—*pitch* (nose-up/nose-down), *roll* (wingtip-up/wingtip-down), and *yaw* (nose-left/nose-right).

While it had become clear to Lockheed that a multifaceted air vehicle would present a highly reduced RCS to enemy radar networks, it was not immediately known how to make an unstable aircraft perform well in the air—and stability, for any airborne weapons delivery platform, is a key requirement for accuracy. Yet Lockheed was convinced that it could develop and produce a viable stealth aircraft that would be stable and could defeat current and projected radar networks, ground-to-air and air-to-air radar-guided and heat-seeking missiles, and fighter aircraft with look-down/shoot-down radar systems. Working closely with the Department of Defense (DOD)—specifically, its Defense Advanced Research Projects Agency (DARPA) and the U.S. Air Force's Aeronautical Systems Division (ASD)—the Lockheed Advanced Development Company (LADC), the Skunk Works, set wheels in motion to quickly develop and field a LO, or stealth, air vehicle with unprecedented survivability and a precision weapon delivery capability.

Before the USAF established a weapon system program office (WSPO) for a LO air vehicle, General Alton D. Slay, who later became commander of Air Force Systems Command (AFSC), was made LO Air Vehicle Program Manager. Reporting to Gen. Slay, five dedicated USAF staff officers defined a high-priority specific operational requirement (SOR) for a LO air vehicle. Then an LO air vehicle WSPO was established within ASD with minimal need-to-know personnel, headed by the late Gen. (then Colonel) Dave Englund. Simultaneously, under the direction of Norm Nelson, a similar team was formed within the Lockheed Skunk Works. Program security headed the list of project priorities.

The Lockheed and U.S. Air Force low-observable stealth air vehicle program offices were supported by other groups and organizations whose efforts were critical to the secret project. These entities included: 1) The U.S. Air Force Office of Special Investigations, which developed and maintained workable security measures on the program; 2) The Air Force Logistics Command (AFLC), specifically, its Sacramento Air Logistics Center at McClellan AFB, California, which was responsible for provision of secure, specialized logistical support, including supply support of all government furnished equipment; and 3) The Tactical Air Command (TAC), which worked closely with the low-observable stealth air vehicle WSPO and Lockheed to initially define the SOR, then establish a secure, full maintenance and operational capability at Tonopah Test Range Airfield in the Nellis AFB test range complex (restricted area R4809). Moreover, a large number of subcontractors were assembled to work in concert with Lockheed and the LO air vehicle WSPO.

## Lockheed: The Stealthy Choice

Almost from the outset, because of its vast experience in aircraft programs of covert nature, Lockheed was the single-source airframe contractor. In other words, there was not a formal competition between rival airframe contractors on the stealth fighter program. However, though lacking details, there might have been an early competition between Lockheed and Northrop to win the Have Blue experimental survivable testbed air vehicle manufacturing rights (to be discussed later). It has been reported though not confirmed that both Lockheed and Northrop built scale models of their respective Have Blue designs for pole-mounted radar tests, and that after the "pole" fly-off, Lockheed's design advanced. But this competition, if it came about, has not been verified at this writing.

The Lockheed F-117A stealth fighter was created to defeat the threat Russia and its allies fielded in the early 1970s and subsequent decades. Today, in 1992, there is no known defense against the Black Jet.

# 2

# Developmental Highlights

L ONG BEFORE the Lockheed F-117A became a fully missionized weapon system—or the workhorse it proved to be in Operation Desert Storm—a number of emerging technologies had to be developed concurrently for stealth aircraft applications. These technologies included: much improved ways to measure an aircraft's RCS (radar cross section); electronic emissions from avionics and the IR (infrared) signature; all-digital FBW (fly-by-wire) flight control systems; advanced composite materials for airframe structures (internal and external); advanced ordnance delivery systems for precision-guided weapons; and advanced airframe design and manufacturing processes via CAD (computer-aided design) and CAM (computer-aided manufacturing) or CAD/CAM. And, to actually create a viable stealth aircraft—specifically, an in-weather strike fighter—LO (low-observable) technology had to be demonstrated and validated (dem /val) by a manned experimental survivable testbed (XST) air vehicle. To do this in total secrecy, a highly classified program code named Have Blue was initiated. Only those personnel with the "need to know" about the secret program received clearances.

## Have Blue

The Lockheed Skunk Works, recognized for its leadership on covert aircraft programs and stealthy aircraft (refer to Chapter 5), was selected to be the single-source airframe contractor on the Have Blue XST program on 1 November 1975. At that time, the U.S. Air Force (USAF) and Defense Advanced Research Projects Agency (DARPA) awarded Lockheed a contract to design, develop, build, flight-test, and evaluate two XST air vehicles by using, for the most part, off-the-shelf components including an in-production powerplant. The first example was to dem/val the type's flying characteristics, while the number two air vehicle was to dem/val the type's signatures—or, hopefully, lack thereof.

Much as the Manhattan Project of World War II, which gave birth to the atomic bomb, the Have Blue program was to remain classified throughout its life cycle. This objective was accomplished, in fact, the Have Blue program was not declassified by the Department of Defense (DOD) until April 1991. (DARPA was founded on 7 February 1958 as ARPA [Advanced Research Projects Agency], a special branch of the DOD chartered to develop high-risk aerospace technologies with potentially high benefits; ARPA was renamed DARPA in the early 1970s.)

To manufacture its two Have Blue XST dem/val aircraft, Lockheed's criterion, in part, was as follows:

- Build them small and light—about one-third the actual size of a production aircraft.
- Employ a single-seat cockpit with an ejection seat.
- Employ as many off-the-shelf aircraft components as possible to speed development time and reduce cost.
- Employ two non-augmented (non-afterburning) General Electric J85 turbojet engines.
- Employ no tactical equipment (i.e., IFF [Identification friend or foe], inflight refueling capability, weapons bay, etc.).
- Produce improved RAM (radar absorbing material) for external application and a better way to apply it.

Already designed, it was time to build the two Have Blue XST air vehicles. Lockheed's design for the XST was unlike any aircraft seen before. Instead of curves, it had angles. It had two vertical tails canted inward toward each other. Its powerplants were mounted atop its wings, and its wings were of a semi-delta planform. It looked more like Captain Nemo's submarine, the *Nautilus*, than an airplane, but if all came about as planned, its shape alone promised to reduce its RCS by as much as 85 percent!

Literally built by hand without permanent jigs, Lockheed workers secretly assembled the two Have Blue XST aircraft in a cordoned-off area within Lockheed's Plant 10 facility at USAF Plant 42, Palmdale, California. Neither air vehicle received USAF serial numbers nor a DOD designation. Lockheed, however, gave its own serial numbers to the aircraft—1001 and 1002, meaning Plant 10, airframes one and two.

As previously discussed, the Have Blue XST air vehicles were small and light. They came with 22-foot wingspans, 38-foot lengths (without nose booms), and a height of $7^1/_2$ feet; gross weight was 12,000 pounds. The leading edges of their semi-delta wings were swept aftward 72.5 degrees (five degrees more than the F-117A's 67.5 degrees), and instead of outward-canted twin vertical tails, they featured twin vertical tails canted 30 degrees inward from the vertical; these were swept back 35 degrees at their leading edges. They incorporated Northrop F-5 landing gear, cockpit instrumentation, and ejection seats. Maximum speed was Mach 0.80 and endurance was one hour. Their wings featured two inboard trailing edge elevons for pitch and roll control, their all-movable rudders provided yaw control, and four lift-dump spoilers (two on top of the wing and two on bottom) were mounted just forward of the elevons.

For comparison, the XST air vehicles were some 21 feet narrower, 5 feet lower, 28 feet shorter, and 40,500 pounds lighter than the production F-117A, but, generally similar

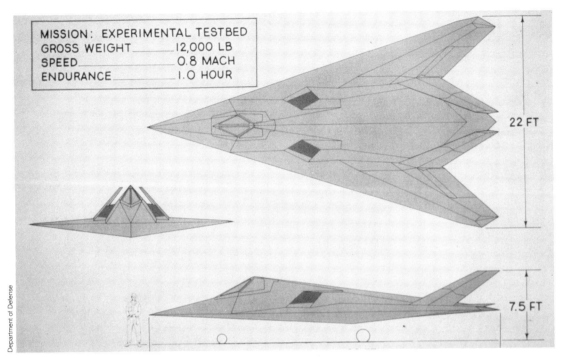

MISSION: EXPERIMENTAL TESTBED
GROSS WEIGHT_____12,000 LB
SPEED_____0.8 MACH
ENDURANCE_____1.0 HOUR

22 FT

7.5 FT

*Have Blue general arrangement.*

*Rare photo of Have Blue. In its camouflage paint, it's pretty stealthy visually, too!*

in overall appearance. Have Blue aircraft, however, employed V-type windscreens (a la F-102/F-106) while the F-117A uses a three-piece flat plate windshield.

The number one Have Blue XST air vehicle was finished in November 1977, two years after program go-ahead. It was subsequently loaded (wings removed) aboard a Lockheed C-5A Galaxy transport and flown to a highly classified flight test area in the

Nellis test range complex. Earlier, Lockheed selected William M. (Bill) Park to serve as chief test pilot on the Have Blue program. The U.S. Air Force chose Lt. Col. Norman Kenneth (Ken) Dyson to serve as USAF project pilot on the Have Blue program. (At this writing, Dyson is chief test pilot at Rockwell's North American Aircraft, flying the X-31.)

Lockheed equipped both Have Blue XST aircraft with fly-by-wire (FBW) flight control systems from the F-16 which were modified to make the aircraft stable about all three axes (the F-16 is only unstable about the pitch axis). The two XST air vehicles have the distinction of being some of the smallest and lightest aircraft ever flown by man. They were not glamorous—but glamor was not one of their requirements.

*Seated pilot provides good size reference in this rare Have Blue photo.*

After its arrival, assembly, and systems checks, the first XST air vehicle completed a series of low- and medium-speed taxi trials. Then, in December 1977, Bill Park made its successful first flight. Flight-testing proceeded better than expected for about four months, considering the type's inherent instability; excellent piloting and the F-16's modified fly-by-wire FCS (flight control system) made the difference. As had been predicted during wind tunnel evaluations, the XST air vehicle had a very high landing speed due to its lack of flaps or speed brakes—about 160 knots.

Following yet another successful test hop on 4 May 1978, flight test 36, Bill Park attempted to make a landing. But, as fate would have it, the aircraft reminded everyone about its high landing speed. As it occurred, one of the XST's main landing gears (it has not been clarified which one) hit the runway too hard. The force of impact caused it to move into a half-extended/half-retracted configuration. Park made several attempts to free the jammed gear by impacting the other main landing gear onto the runway. He hoped to free up the jammed gear in this fashion so that it would either retract for a possible belly landing, or extend for a normal landing—but to no avail. He could make neither a normal wheels-down nor emergency wheels-up landing. Thus he was instructed to climb to a safe altitude for emergency bailout.

After blowing the canopy, Park ejected, but somehow hit his head and was knocked unconscious. He was still unconscious when he hit the ground, and since he was unable to control his parachute descent or landing, he sustained severe back injuries on impact—severe enough, unfortunately, that he had to take an early retirement from flying. But Park stayed on at Lockheed and became head of Flight Test Operations, a position he held until his retirement in 1990.

Have Blue XST air vehicle number one, then—the flight test and evaluation (FT&E) airplane—was a total loss. It was secretly disposed of somewhere in the Nellis test range complex. Have Blue XST air vehicle number two—the LO or stealth testbed—arrived shortly after the demise of number one. Its first flight, with Lt. Col. Dyson at the controls, occurred in June 1978.

Have Blue XST number one proved that a faceted airplane could indeed fly, but it was up to Have Blue XST number two to dem/val that the type could truly survive—that is, fly against various radar systems (ground-to-air, air-to-air, and air-to-ground) and present such a tiny RCS that it would not be detected by these radar systems. In addition, it had to undergo IR and electronic emission detection tests.

During 52 LO or stealth dem/val flights, flown between June 1978 and July 1979, the type proved its survivability. Then, during flight number 52 in July 1979, XST number two was lost.

As it happened, one of its non-afterburning J85 turbojet engines caught fire (it is not clear which one), and the subsequent fire grew intense enough to burn through some of the hydraulic fluid lines. With a fire on board that could not be extinguished, and with the loss of hydraulic power, Dyson was cleared to abandon the aircraft. He made a successful emergency ejection and a good parachute landing. But, like XST number one, XST number two was a total loss.

There was no need to build any additional Have Blue-type air vehicles at that point, since the first of five FSD or full scale development Senior Trend aircraft would soon be under construction.


## Senior Trend

Following its submission of two LO or stealth technology aircraft-type proposals—one resembling the F-117A of today, the other a midsize bomber about the size of a B-58—Lockheed was awarded a go-ahead FSD contract on the Senior Trend program in November 1978. It was to produce five FSD examples of the former rather than the latter (the latter having a two-man crew and four engines, but otherwise very similar to the F-117A configuration). The Senior Trend FSD aircraft are essentially pre-production-type F-117A air vehicles that were (are) used for early FT&E, LO, and weapon delivery tests; two are still being used for ongoing tests, two are not accounted for and one (number two) has been delivered to the Air Force Museum (AFM) at Wright-Patterson AFB, Dayton, Ohio.

To manufacture the five Senior Trend FSD F-117A aircraft, besides increasing size and weight values, a number of revisions and additions had to be engineered and employed. These, in part, included:

- Reengineered cockpit and cockpit canopy.
- Redesigned twin vertical tails.
- Revision of the powerplant system; revision of the air inlets and exhaust outlets.
- Application of LO air data probes.
- Incorporation of a weapons bay, weapons racks, and weapons delivery systems.

- Employment of new and off-the-shelf tactical avionics.
- Addition of a parachute braking system and arresting hook.
- Incorporation of a "wet wing" in the fuel system.
- Addition of an anti-icing engine air inlet wiper blade system.
- Employment of retractable antennas, inflight refueling receptacle, and formation and anti-collision lights.
- Application of improved LO or stealth technologies as they were made.

In early June 1981, the first Senior Trend FSD F-117A airplane was delivered via C-5A. After having its wings attached, it was prepared for FT&E. Lockheed chose Harold C. (Hal) Farley to serve as chief test pilot on the Senior Trend program.

On 18 June 1981, Hal Farley made a successful first flight on the number one FSD F-117A. During mid-1981 and early 1982, the other four FSD F-117As were successfully flown. All went well until April 1982, when the first production Senior Trend F-117A arrived. It was ready for its first flight on 20 April.

On that day, in preparation for the first flight of the first production F-117A, Lockheed test pilot Robert L. (Bob) Riedenauer lined up for takeoff. But unknown to him (or anyone else, apparently), some cables that operate the aircraft's flying control surfaces had been installed incorrectly (i.e., pitch was yaw and vice versa). Riedenauer advanced the throttles, released the brakes, and powered forward to rotation speed and takeoff. The airplane rotated as planned, but immediately after liftoff, just after the main landing gear cleared the runway, the airplane went beserk. Instead of the nose pitching upward, it yawed horizontally and loss of control was instantaneous. There was no time for Riedenauer to correct the errant action of the airplane nor to eject from it. Just seconds after rotation, the airplane flew into the ground. Bob Riedenauer was injured severely, and, after recovery, was forced to retire from flying. The first production F-117A was damaged beyond repair, and since it crashed before delivery, it was not accepted; some parts were salvaged.

## Initial Operational Capability

The 4450th Tactical Group (TG), which had been secretly established in 1979 as the sole operator of the F-117A, under the command of Col. Robert J. (Bob) Jackson, achieved initial operational capability (IOC) on 28 October 1983 with the acceptance of production F-117A number 14; at this time, however, the 4450th TG was under the command of Col. James S. Allen. Continued operations, all of which occurred at night, went relatively smoothly until 11 July 1986.

On that night, while flying production F-117A number eight, Maj. Ross E. Mulhare crashed into a mountain located about 17 miles northeast of Bakersfield, California. Major Mulhare was killed, apparently making no attempt to eject, and his aircraft was destroyed by the impact. A definite cause was not publicly disclosed, but disorientation is a strong possibility.

A second crash occurred on 14 October 1987. On that night, while flying production F-117A number 31, Maj. Michael C. Stewart crashed in the Nellis ranges. He too was killed and apparently made no attempt to eject. Once again, the official cause was not disclosed; disorientation was again a likely cause.

Those two crashes, along with the need to better integrate the F-117A into its operational plans, forced the U.S. Air Force to initiate daytime as well as nighttime flying missions. To accomplish this, since the stealth fighter is not invisible, its existence had to be publicly disclosed. This announcement was scheduled to occur in early 1988, but internal Pentagon pressure forced a 10-month delay.

Lockheed

*The first F-117A photograph ever shown to the general public.*

But finally, following years of media speculation that a stealth fighter did exist, Defense Department spokesman Dan Howard held a press conference on 10 November 1988 at the Pentagon. There, with the official release of a single poor-quality photograph and very few details, the actual existence of the long-rumored stealth fighter was verified.

Surprisingly, the airplane was not at all curvaceous, as had been assumed. Instead, it was just the opposite—quite angular. All previous artists' concepts and a good-selling model kit depicting the elusive aircraft became obsolete in an instant.

The aircraft's official designation, assumed to be F-19, was in fact F-117A—a complete surprise! Since there was no airplane with the designation of F-19 between the McDonnell Douglas F-18 and the Northrop F-20, this had been a logical assumption. The F-117 designation was a good ploy, too, because after the General Dynamics F-111, there were no more Century-series designations issued to fighter aircraft.

In retrospect, about the only thing that was *not* a surprise was the fact that the stealth fighter was a product of the Lockheed Skunk Works. The U.S. Air Force, whose number one priority had been program security since day number one, has to be congratulated for keeping its stealth fighter program secret for more than a decade!

*The planform of the F-117A (tail number 804) is shown to good advantage in this spectacular view. Tail code WA (for Nellis AFB) is noteworthy.*

The 4450th TG was disestablished in October 1989, and at the same time, its successor, the 37th Tactical Fighter Wing (TFW), was established. The 4450th TG, when disestablished, had three fighter squadrons. These were: Squadron One, the Night Stalkers; Squadron Two, the Grim Reapers; and Squadron Three (no known nickname). Squadrons One and Two operated production F-117As, while Squadron Three operated the five preproduction FSD F-117As and, for chase and training, some LTV (Ling-Temco-Vought) A-7Ds. This strange mix of aircraft was maintained for a while after the formation of the 37th TFW; however, T-38A and AT-38B aircraft replaced the A-7Ds. Moreover, the three squadrons (One, Two, and Three) were soon redesignated as the 415th, 416th, and 417th respectively.

The 415th Tactical Fighter Squadron (TFS) kept Squadron One's nickname, the Night Stalkers. However, the 416th TFS and the 417th Tactical Fighter Training Squadron (TFTS) did not keep their predecessor's nicknames. The 416th TFS was nicknamed the Ghost Riders, while the 417th TFTS became the Bandits. At the time, the 37th TFW was under the command of Col. Anthony J. (Tony) Tolin.

A giant aerospace media event occurred on 21 April 1990 at both Nellis AFB and the Pentagon, when the Defense Department released more details on the F-117A, 10 still photographs of good quality, and an eight-minute video. Simultaneously, at Nellis, two F-117A aircraft were publicly displayed. At this time, the 37th TFW had 56 operational F-117As on hand, with only one more airplane to be delivered and accepted. This came about on 12 July 1990 at Lockheed's Plant 10 facility at Air Force Plant 42, when the last production F-117A was delivered to the U.S. Air Force in Palmdale, California.

*The five full-scale development F-117A aircraft are nearly identical to the 59 production F-117As. This is the number 4 full-scale development F-117A (tail number 783), photographed at an Edwards AFB open house.*

## Flying the F-117A

Flying the F-117A, according to pilot reports, is a pleasure. It is easy to fly and not a "Woblin' Goblin" by current measures, although early on, its nose had a tendency to "hunt" (i.e., oscillate). It is said to handle very much like a McDonnell Douglas F-15, which, like the F-117, has light wing loading and is very maneuverable. The F-117, however, due to its design, has a normal sink rate but a high landing speed which compares to that of the F-106—about 160-plus knots or 240-plus miles per hour. It is for this reason, in part, that the F-117 has such a large braking and/or drag parachute (about 18 feet in diameter). Its parabrake is deployed as soon as the nosewheel makes contact with the runway. This action helps to slow the fast-moving aircraft down and eliminate excessive wear on the wheel brakes. The drag parachute also doubles as an antispin device if the aircraft should ever enter spin—a most unwanted activity.

Early on, before a pilot could solo on the F-117A, he had to take F-15 training and practice a number of no-flap landings before the real thing in an F-117A. That activity, however, is no longer a requirement for prospective pilots because of much improved F-117 cockpit simulators.

Another flying pleasure for F-117 pilots is its hallmark General Electric F404 turbo-

*Production F-117A number 23 (tail number 807) at Tonopah.*

fan engine. It is responsive and reliable, and it has adequate thrust for the F-117's high subsonic speed regime (0.80 Mach number).

The F-117A's flying surfaces include four elevons (two inboard/two outboard) on the trailing edge of either wing, and two all-movable rudders (one atop either fixed vertical tail stub). The four elevons deflect upward and downward about 60 degrees, and the two rudders deflect left and right about 30 degrees; deflection is quite fast. The elevons are split into four segments because of their area (size) and do not act as flaps; they operate as two elevons (one on the trailing edge of either wing) in flight. The all-movable rudders are one piece and each pivots on a single post protruding from either vertical tail stub. The elevons act in the pitch and roll axes, while the rudders act in the yaw axis. To help reduce the aircraft's high landing speed, its runway approach and landing touchdown angle of attack (AOA) is $9^1/2$ degrees. The aircraft's flat bottom is not based on the lifting body theory, as has been reported in other references, but is for LO characteristics only.

The mission of the F-117A is to strike and destroy high-value targets, in a precise manner, with any conventional or nuclear device that can fit within the aircraft's internal weapons bay. Strategic targets such as radar installations, command and control bunkers, hardened aircraft hangars, and surface-to-surface and surface-to-air guided missile sites are amongst the Black Jet's primary prey. It can carry and deliver precision-guided ordnance in weather, specifically during nighttime. Located in its belly on centerline, the F-117A's internal weapons bay has two inboard-opening doors. The weapons bay is long,

*Inflight shot of production F-117A number 12 (tail number 796).*

wide, and deep enough to provide an adequate internal volume for a variety of tactical ordnance. Some known tactical devices that are carried by the F-117A include:

- Two laser-guided MK84 2,000-pound bombs.
- Two laser-guided GBU-10 Paveway II 2,000-pound bombs.
- Two laser-guided GBU-12 Paveway II 500-pound bombs.
- Two laser-guided GBU-27 Paveway III 2,000-pound bombs; these are BLU-109/B "improved" 2,000-pound bombs (MK84s) with the Paveway III guidance system.
- Nuclear devices (unspecified); all Tactical Air Command fighter aircraft are capable of carrying/delivering nuclear devices.

The F-117A is not optimized for contemporary self-defense. That is, it has neither cannon nor air-to-air guided missiles for its own protection. Instead, it simply relies on its LO technology for its survival when in action. This was proved on a day-to-day basis during Operation Desert Storm, and its continual tactical surprise during that period was due for the most part to the extreme difficulties any defense has in detecting such a beast. And, as now proved, its laser-guided bombs strike with extreme accuracy.

The F-117A is not only a deadly warplane, it is an award-winner. In 1988, Benjamin R. (Ben) Rich (retired "chief skunk" and consultant to the Skunk Works) as well as the entire Lockheed and U.S. Air Force F-117A team received the prestigious Collier Trophy for the "Greatest Achievement in Aeronautics and Astronautics in America." Also in

**15**

*Overhead view of an F-117A.*

*Last F-117A airplane delivered (tail number 844).*

1988, the 4450th TG (now the 37th TFW), was awarded the Tactical Air Command Commander's Maintenance Award in the Special Mission Category.

In September 1989, three of the F-117A's main creators—Alan Brown (former Skunk Works director of technology and now Lockheed Corporation director of engineering), Norm Nelson (retired Skunk Works vice president and general manager), and Dick Cantrell (former Skunk Works director of technology and now senior advisor on the F-22 ATF [Advanced Tactical Fighter] program)—received the design award of the American Institute of Aeronautics and Astronautics. Finally, the 37th TFW has earned superior ratings during Operational Readiness Inspections.

These awards are sure to be followed by others. And these awards, in part, give credit to the clever engineers and hard workers that teamed up to create such a unique airplane—the Lockheed F-117A Black Jet, the world's first stealth fighter.

# 3

# Airframe and Powerplant Systems and Structures

THE LOCKHEED F-117A Black Jet incorporates unique airframe and powerplant systems and structures. These systems and structures work in concert to allow the stealth fighter to operate in a war zone with near-impunity. This was fully demonstrated during Operation Desert Storm.

## Cockpit and Canopy

The F-117A cockpit/canopy configuration is the result of clever engineering and comments from experienced pilots during the design and development stages. The cockpit is user-friendly, and, except for side-to-side headroom, is relatively comfortable. The cockpit is covered by a large and heavy (about 400 pounds) hood-like canopy with five flat transparencies for external viewing (one on either side, three in front). The F-117A pilot sits on a standard McDonnell Douglas ACES II ejection seat as employed by F-15C/D Eagles, and he controls the aircraft via a center-mounted control stick between his legs.

The cockpit is situated far forward on the aircraft and provides good visibility 90 degrees left and right; however, forward, up, down, and rear visibility are impaired. The canopy ceiling (which has no transparency for outside viewing) and the wing leading edges cause blind spots, and over-the-nose visibility is poor. The F-117A pilot, looking aft over his shoulders, is hard pressed to see either wingtip, and he sits so high over a short, pointed nose that he feels as if he is riding the tip of a dart.

The five flat plate panels in the one-piece canopy are specially treated to further reduce the aircraft's already low RCS. Two heavy-duty actuators, one on either side of the cockpit, raise and lower the hood-like canopy which has three locking devices on either

*Good view of F-117A cockpit. Spiked edges are notable.*

side. If an emergency should arise, the F-117 pilot would jettison the cockpit canopy and exit his aircraft by way of the rocket-powered ACES II zero-speed/zero-altitude ejection seat for an automated parachute descent to safety.

## Digital Fly-by-Wire Flight Control System

The F-117A is equipped with an all-digital fly-by-wire flight control system. It is quadruple-redundant, and, except for computer software, is similar to the flight control system employed by the General Dynamics F-16C/D Fighting Falcon. Since the F-117A is inherently unstable about all three axes (pitch, roll, and yaw), it simply could not fly and maneuver as well as it does without its excellent fly-by-wire flight control system.

## Tactical Cockpit Displays

To reduce development time and overall program cost, the F-117A employs many new and off-the-shelf tactical cockpit displays, most of which are borrowed from the McDonnell Douglas F/A-18C/D Hornet. Honeywell provides the radar altimeter, INS (Inertial Navigation System), ADC (Air Data Computer), and the CMD (Color Multipurpose Display). Harris provides the Digital Moving Map Radar, while Kaiser provides the PIU (Projection Interface Unit) and the PDU (Projection Display Unit). The three tactical cockpit displays (left, center, and right) are 1) the left-hand DDI or Digital Display Indicator; 2) the cen-

*F-117A's large clamshell-style canopy.*

ter-mounted Horizontal Indicator; and 3) the right-hand DDI. The F-117's HUD (Head-up Display) is a modified F-15C/D Eagle unit.

## Internal Weapons Bay

The F-117A's internal weapons bay has two wells (left/right); these are covered by two doors that open inboard toward centerline and close outboard toward the wingtips. The outer edges of the weapons bay doors have diamond-shaped bumpers that prevent damage to the doors when they are opened. The weapons bay has enough volume to house up to 5,000 pounds of ordnance (up to 2,500 pounds in either well), and is optimized to carry either conventional or nuclear freefall and guided bombs. To allow for clean ordnance drops, and to reduce buffet when the weapons bay doors are open, there are four small spoilers (two on either side) just forward of the retractable weapons racks. The two weapons racks (one in either well) are lowered and raised via hydraulic fluid pressure. The F-117A cannot carry any external ordnance at all, as this would defeat its LO or stealth purpose.

## Propulsion System

For propulsion, the F-117A relies on what is truly a hallmark powerplant, the General Electric (GE) F404 turbofan engine. For operation at high subsonic speed (0.80 Mach number, maximum), the stealth fighter employs two non-augmented (non-afterburning)

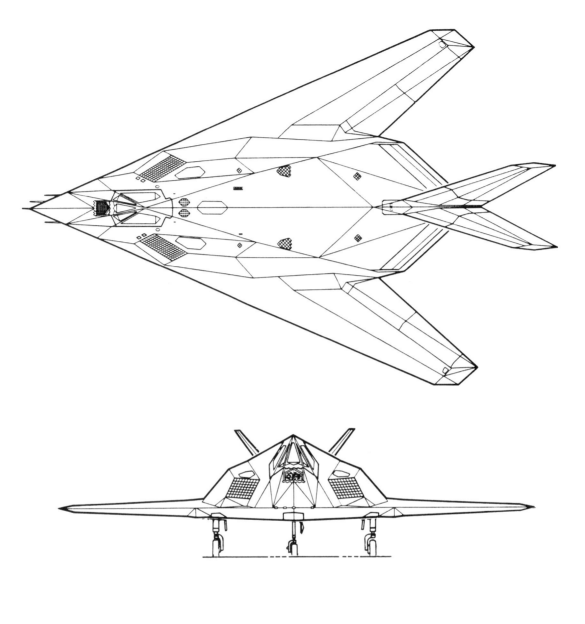

*F-117A's unique faceted configuration.*

Lockheed

*F-117A pilots ride on the apex of the semi-delta wing.*

*Two F-117A's (numbers 793 and 832) at Tonopah Test Range Airfield.*

F404-GE-F1D2 engines. The F404-GE-F1D2 is a derivative of the afterburning F404-GE-400 turbofan that powers several successful aircraft including the McDonnell Douglas F/A-18 Hornet (for which the F404 was originally developed), the Grumman X-29A Forward Swept Wing Advanced Technology Demonstrator, and the Rockwell/MBB X-31A Enhanced Fighter Maneuverability airplane.

Lockheed's choice of the GE F404 turbofan for the F-117A was not by chance. There is a basic rule of thumb within the ranks of aerospace engineers which is as follows: The airframe can be only as good as the powerplant that propels it. Another rule of thumb on the development of a successful airframe has five parts: The powerplant selected should be small, light, reliable, and have an excellent engine-thrust-to-weight ratio and exceptional specific fuel consumption. The F404 met Lockheed's criteria and it became the engine of choice rather than chance.

The history of the GE F404 turbofan engine dates back to 1971 when, with Defense Department permission, the General Electric Company announced the existence of its Model GE15, later designated YJ101-GE-100. As advertised, the J101 was an advanced afterburning 15,000-pound thrust class turbojet engine, which had been specifically tailored to the propulsion system requirement of the proposed P-530 Cobra, a privately funded Northrop project. As proposed by Northrop, the P-530 Cobra was to be a high-performance, twin-engine, single-seat lightweight multi-role fighter airplane with empha-

*General Electric F404-GE-F1D2 turbofan engine.*

*F404-GE-F1D2 engine.*

sis on the air superiority role. It was to meet the defense need of America's allies at low cost, and would be used for close support, interdiction, photographic reconnaissance, and high-speed aerial intercept missions. In essence, the P-530 was to be be the replacement for Northrop's own F-5 series. But the Northrop Cobra was never produced.

*General Electric YJ101-GE-100 turbojet engine, the forerunner of the hallmark F404 series.*

The USAF, however, liked the J101 engine so well that it awarded GE a full-scale development contract in 1972 for a number of applications—specifically, air superiority fighters—during the 1975 to 1990 time period.

Following the demise of the Northrop P-530 Cobra project, the first application of the GE J101 was with the new Northrop P-630 LWF or lightweight fighter prototype, the YF-17, the first of two examples first flying on 9 June 1974. Amazingly, just 14 days after the maiden flight of the premier YF-17, it achieved supersonic speed in level flight. More importantly, it did this *without* using the afterburners on its two GE YJ101-GE-100 engines! This particular feat was a milestone in aviation history, and went unmatched until the advent of the four ATF (Advanced Tactical Fighter) prototypes in 1990, which were specifically designed to fly supersonically without using their respective afterburners!

Although the Northrop YF-17 lost the LWF competition to the General Dynamics YF-16, development of the J101 moved forward—but not as a turbojet engine, but rather a turbo*fan* to boost thrust and lower specific fuel consumption while keeping its reliability, small size, and low weight. This continued development process led to the creation of the afterburning 16,000-pound thrust class F404-GE-400 turbofan engine to propel the McDonnell Douglas/Northrop F/A-18 Hornet, a larger and heavier version of the YF-17 for the U.S. Navy, U.S. Marines, and U.S. allies. The first F/A-18 made its first flight on 18 November 1978, which, incidentally, was also the approximate date that Lockheed received the go-ahead for FSD on the Senior Trend (F-117A) program.

Earlier, when Lockheed propulsion engineers began to look for an adequate F-117A

*Proposed Northrop P-530 Cobra.*

*Northrop YF-17 LWF prototype.*

27

*General Electric F404-GE-400 turbofan engine is similar to F-117A's -F1D2 engine, but with an afterburner section.*

propulsion system, they set their sights on a non-afterburning version of the GE F404 turbofan engine, as it could be easily produced and would be available when needed. Thus, working secretly in concert, Lockheed and General Electric came up with the powerplant for the first LO technology aircraft in the world.

*McDonnell Douglas/Northrop F/A-18A Hornet.*

Actual development on the non-afterburning turbofan engine, the GE F404-GE-F1D2, for the Lockheed F-117A began in 1980. The first production engine was delivered to and accepted by the USAF in 1981; final delivery and acceptance occurred in 1990.

Counting spares, GE most probably produced some 200 -F1D2 engines for the F-117A program. Moreover, if required, GE maintains the capability of producing additional -F1D2 engines.

Generically, General Electric says the -F1D2 version of its F404 turbofan engine is in the 10,000-pound thrust class. It has a maximum envelope length of 87 inches (7.25 feet), a maximum envelope diameter of 35 inches (2.916 feet), and a dry weight of 1,730 pounds.

Like all versions of the F404, whether augmented or not, the F-117A's F404-GE-F1D2 is of modular construction and incorporates a fan module, a high-pressure compressor module, a combustor module, a high-pressure turbine module, and a low-pressure turbine module. It features line-replaceable units or LRUs which are located for easy access through engine bay doors on the F-117A, as well as borescope ports that enable the inspection of internal parts while the engine remains installed within the airplane. Reportedly, one F404-GE-F1D2 can be removed from an F-117A and another installed in about one hour.

*F-117A's unique engine air inlets.*

The General Electric F404 turbofan is an excellent powerplant indeed, but this was not known when Lockheed chose it to propel the F-117A. Once again, the Lockheed Skunk Works demonstrated a great deal of foresight when it selected the F404 for the F-117's propulsion system—and foresight is one quality that is not a rule of thumb.

## Engine Air Inlet System

Another unique feature of the F-117A is its engine air inlet system. Except for the two Have Blue XST aircraft, it is of a type never seen before on any air vehicle.

*Suck-in doors atop engine nacelles provide additional air during low-speed operations.*

Each engine air inlet (one on either side of the fuselage) has two grated covers with a large number of rectangular openings. Each cover has 46 horizontal openings and 36 vertical openings for a total of 1,656 openings in the four covers on each F-117A. These tiny openings, of course, restrict airflow to the engines, especially when taxiing. Moreover, any buildup of ice can restrict airflow even further. Therefore, while taxiing, two large-area auxiliary air inlets, one atop each engine nacelle, open inward to increase the airflow to the engines. To eliminate ice buildups, the F-117 employs a wiper blade system that removes ice during flight; a light on either side of the fuselage illuminates the engine air inlet covers at night so pilots can see the operation in action. The air ducts run straight to the faces of the engines from the inlet covers. Thus, there is no so-called "snaking" of the engine air ducts.

## Engine Exhaust Outlet System

The F-117A's engine exhaust outlet system is likewise unique. The exhaust outlets, one on either side of centerline, are mounted atop the wing chord plane, as are the air inlets. They

*Ice wiper blades are located just forward and below the air inlets on either side of the fuselage. Note FLIR and inflight refueling receptacle.*

are narrow and wide to present as low an infrared (heat) signature as possible, and they are masked from the rear and bottom by the F-117's so-called platypus bill-shaped aft fuselage section. There are 12 grated openings on either side of the fuselage that are designed to scatter the aircraft's exhaust pattern. Each of the total of 24 exhaust orifices measures about six inches square. The exhaust pipes are rounded at the rear of the F404 engines, and become flume-like at the front of the exhaust outlets. Planning is underway to modify these exhaust outlets for improved stealth characteristics and easier maintenance. Although the system works well, Lockheed has said that the exhaust has caused more problems than any other system on the airplane.

*F-117A's unique engine exhaust outlets (left-hand shown).*

## Flying Control Surfaces

The F-117A's flying control surfaces consist of two rudders and two two-segment elevons. The rudders are located atop each vertical tail stub and provide yaw. The elevons are located at the trailing edge of the semi-delta wings and provide pitch and roll; there are no flaps. The flying control surfaces are operated by means of a central-mount control stick and rudder pedals through the aircraft's all-digital fly-by-wire electronic flight control system. The elevons double as elevators and ailerons and deflect 60 degrees up and down. The all-movable rudders deflect 30 degrees left and right. The speed of deflection of all control surfaces is reportedly quite fast.

## Landing Gear and Parachute Braking Systems

The landing gear and parachute braking systems of the Black Jet are products of Menasco and Pioneer, respectively. The landing gear is of standard tricycle type with single wheels and tires that retract forward; the gear doors have serrated edges to help reduce the aircraft's RCS. The braking parachute, or parabrake, is located under split doors atop the aft

*Upswept boattail hides exhaust outlets from below and rear.*

*F-117A's trailing edge wing elevons.*

fuselage section; these open outboard to deploy the parachute. The large-diameter parachute (about 18 feet) is designed to reduce wear on the carbon brakes and slow the aircraft's rollout speed after landing touchdown. It is deployed as soon as the nose gear contacts the runway.

*F-117A's all-movable rudder assembly.*

James Goodall via Tony Landis

## Fuselage, Wing, and Tail Structures

The fuselage, wing, and tail structures of the F-117A are a mixture of metal alloys and composite materials—about 95 percent metal, 5 percent composite.

The F-117A's fuselage is of conventional semi-monocoque all-metal construction—mostly aluminum alloy. The aircraft's faceted external surfaces attach directly to the subframe and without blending. A special—and secret—radar absorbing material (RAM) is employed externally.

The F-117A's wing is of cantilever low-wing monoplane design and is of a semi-delta planform; leading edge sweepback is 67.5 degrees. Like the fuselage, the wing is of all-metal construction. It has trailing edge elevons for pitch and roll control.

The F-117A has two vertical tails that are outboard-canted in a V-tail arrangement that sweeps back 65 degrees. Each tail stub has an all-movable rudder that pivots on posts for yaw control. The F-117A's rudders were originally of all-metal construction; however, these are now being replaced with all-composite material rudders.

*F-117A's tricycle landing gear.*

## FLIR and DLIR Systems

The F-117A is equipped with forward-looking infrared (FLIR) and downward-looking infrared (DLIR) systems provided by Texas Instruments. The FLIR sensor is located in a recess just ahead of the cockpit windscreen, and is covered by a RAM mesh screen. The DLIR sensor and laser designator is located under the forward fuselage and to the right-hand side of the nose landing gear well; it is also covered by a RAM mesh screen. The F-117A's FLIR and DLIR systems are similar to those used by the F/A-18 Hornet.

## Modifications and Retrofits

Although the Lockheed F-117A Black Jet has been operational for nine years, and is a fully missionized weapon system, there are a number of modifications and retrofits that are either under way or planned to enhance its operability and maintainability, and to lower the cost of support. These modifications and/or retrofits are broad in scope and are not to correct any F-117A shortcomings. These are as follows:

*Engine Exhaust Outlet System.* This modification involves the use of new heat shields, improved seals, new airflow paths, and new high-temperature thermal protection "bricks" at the aft edge of the exhaust system. Paul W. Martin, F-117A program manager at LADC (the "Skunk Works"), calls the changes "fairly simple" ones. He says: "The exhaust system handles very hot, very fast-moving air. In contrast to other aircraft, the F-

*F-117A's parabrake.*

117 blows hot air through the airframe structure itself." He added, "The exhaust system was designed 10 years ago, and it has become one of the more burdensome areas on the plane." According to Martin, upgrading the exhaust system will improve maintenance, leading to a reduction of maintenance man-hours per flight hour (MMH/FH), and will not affect the aircraft's infrared signature nor radar cross-section.

*Avionics.* Planned changes to the F-117A's avionics suite include the installation of a ring laser gyro (RLG) and global positioning system (GPS) receiver on the aircraft. The primary inertial navigation system (INS) used currently by the aircraft is the SPN/JEANS. It is a very accurate system also used by B-52G/H bombers, but it is no longer being produced. Martin explains: "Our plan is to achieve a much higher mean time between failure (MTBF) rate with the RLG [ring laser gyro] without sacrificing accuracy." He added: "In addition, support costs for the SPN/JEANS system are rising, since the system no longer is being produced, so we hope to see a reduction in spending because of the changeover to the new equipment."

To give F-117A pilots greater situational awareness, the aircraft's offensive capability is being improved with the addition of Honeywell color multifunction displays with the capability to integrate a Harris digital moving map. Mr. Martin believes this offensive capability improvement program represents one of the first operational uses of a military-qualified digital moving map in a fighter-type aircraft.

The pair of cathode ray tube (CRT)-based color multifunction displays can be used to call up digital moving maps, target photographs, and target identification diagrams. A

*F-117A's external structure.*

liquid crystal display (LCD)-based data entry panel allows the pilot to select 256 avionics functions. This new cockpit equipment is optimized to minimize the chance of pilot disorientation, which is suspected as the cause of two fatal F-117A crashes.

As more and more F-117As are equipped with new cockpits, they will be reintroduced to their previous operational squadrons, calling for changes in pilot training and procedures.

To provide arrival at a precise time over a point or target, automatic engine throttles will be added to the F-117A fleet; none of the seven aircraft equipped with autothrottles and other cockpit improvements thus far (as of early 1991) flew in Operation Desert Storm. Mr. Martin said: "One of the lessons learned from Desert Storm was flexibility— you need to change the aircraft's tasking almost as you are walking to the airplane. So we need to make the mission planning system able to support this."

The automated mission planning system, which was developed by Lockheed in time to be delivered on the first production F-117A airplane in 1981, was perfected by Lockheed with the goal of easing pilot workload when operating the single-seat night fighter/ attack aircraft.

For all-weather missions, the incorporation of low probability of intercept communications equipment and hardware is under consideration, but not yet approved for retrofit.

***Composite Material Rudders****.* Replacement of the twin all-metal rudders with units made of graphite thermoplastic composite material is under way. This modification was dictated in part by the loss of a rudder from an F-117A some five years ago during a train-

*Close up of F-117A's FLIR.*

An F-117A banks left.

Lockheed artist concept of the F-117A.

First public display of the F-117A.

USAF photo by Senior Master Sgt. Bob Wickley

An F-117A at low altitude.

Lockheed photo by Eric Schulzinger and Denny Lombard

A view of an F-117A/KC10A inflight hookup. This photo illustrates comparative sizes of tanker/cargo and fighter/attack aircraft.

An F-117A on landing approach.

The fifty-ninth and last production F-117A airplane as it appeared during its delivery ceremony.

ing flight at Tonopah Test Range Airfield. According to officials, the rudder "fluttered off" during weapons testing when the airplane was in an unusual flight condition with a large side slip while carrying a 2,000-pound store. The aircraft landed safely despite the loss of the rudder. As a result of the incident, some restrictions were placed on the F-117A's angle of attack and maneuver rates until retrofit. Jack S. Gordon, executive vice president of LADC, says the rudder retrofit has been performed on about half the F-117A fleet, and that the program was interrupted by the aircraft's deployment to Saudi Arabia and its action in the Persian Gulf War.

*Landing Gear Wheels, Tires and Brakes.* The F-117A is being fitted with F-15E Strike Eagle-size wheels and tires, and its existing steel brakes are being replaced by carbon-carbon brakes. The maximum energy-absorbing capability of the current steel brakes can be accommodated by the carbon-carbon brakes using only 60 percent of their capacity.

## Planned and Proposed F-117A Improvements

There are 10 planned and proposed F-117A improvements. These are:

- Exhaust system (*see above*); in progress.
- Composite rudders (*see above*); in progress.
- Offensive capability (*see above*); in progress.
- Larger F-15E-size landing gear wheels, tires, and carbon-carbon brakes (*see above*); not in progress.
- A GPS using the antenna from the Lockheed F-22 ATF; not in progress.
- All-weather capability; not in progress.
- Secure, low probability of intercept communications radio (F-117A pilots in Operation Just Cause [Panama] were unable to discuss changes in attack plans); not in progress.
- Upgraded mission computer (four times the input); not in progress.
- A RLG to replace the SPN/JEANS electrostatically suspended gyro; the SPN/JEANS system uses a spinning beryllium ball that comes within five millionths of an inch of being perfectly round (high accuracy, but 400-hour MTBF rate and rising cost are encouraging the USAF to use a RLG with 2,000-hour MTBF rate); not in progress.
- More user-friendly features in F-117A mission on ground; not in progress.

## Radar-Absorbing Material

The F-117A's radar-absorbing material or RAM is applied with a hand-held, spray-type gun called a "Jost gun." This is named after the engineer who designed it, Mr. Paul Jost. It looks somewhat like the radar guns used by police. Certain F-117A crewmembers are specially trained to apply RAM externally in the field by using the "Jost gun." It reportedly applies RAM quite rapidly and in very even layers when needed.

# 4

# Black Jet Operations

UNDER THE COMMAND of Colonel Robert J. (Bob) Jackson, the unit for exclusive Black Jet operations was established in October 1979 as the 4450th Tactical Group (TG). Based at Tonopah Test Range Airfield, 140 miles northwest of Las Vegas, Nevada, in the test ranges of Nellis AFB, the 4450th TG—the Nighthawks—was initially equipped with LTV A-7D Corsair II aircraft as trainers while it prepared to accept its first and subsequent production F-117A stealth fighter aircraft. The Nighthawks received their first production F-117A airplane on 2 September 1982, and on 28 October 1983, with 14 production F-117As on hand, the 4450th TG achieved initial operational capability (IOC).

The 4450th TG reported directly to Headquarters, Tactical Air Command at Langley AFB, Virginia, until 1985. During that year, operational command was transferred to the Tactical Fighter Weapons Center at Nellis AFB.

The F-117A program was operated under very strict security measures to protect low observable technology development in the United States of America. Then, on 10 November 1988, in order to expand operational integration and to allow daytime training flights, the "powers that be" publicly acknowledged the existence of the stealth fighter. Although its existence came as no real surprise, its appearance and designation completely astounded the aviation media. All previously published drawings of the assumed stealth fighter were proven completely inaccurate.

The 4450th TG was disestablished in October 1989. At the same time, the unit was re-established as the 37th Tactical Fighter Wing (TFW), keeping the nickname "Night-hawks." It now came under the operational command of the 12th Air Force, headquartered at Bergstrom AFB, Texas. Simultaneously, the A-7Ds completed their active training

*Front and side views of two F-117As illustrate their complex geometry.*

role in the unit and were replaced by Northrop T-38A and AT-38B Talon aircraft.

There are about 2,500 military members assigned to the 37th TFW, and most of them live within the greater Las Vegas area and commute to and from Tonopah Test Range Airfield via contract commercial aircraft.

The 37th TFW is currently made up of three squadrons: the 415th TFS, the Night Stalkers; the 416th TFS, the Ghost Riders; and the 417th TFTS, the Bandits. On 17 August 1990, Colonel Alton C. (Al) Whitley, Jr., became the current commander of the 37th TFW. Since replacing Colonel Anthony J. (Tony) Tolin, he has successfully directed the wing's activities during the Persian Gulf War; he flew 19 combat sorties during Operation Desert Storm.

The 37th TFW is scheduled to move to Holloman AFB, New Mexico. Construction of its new facility began in late 1991, and the unit's initial transfer is to begin sometime in 1992. Since Holloman AFB is much more open to the public, the F-117 will become a more familiar sight at its new home. At this writing, however, many details related to the airplane and its operations are still classified—and its current home remains closed to the general public.

As previously mentioned, the 4450th TG (now 37th TFW) had achieved IOC in October 1983. At about the same time, the U.S. Armed Forces and U.S. Caribbean allies invaded the island nation of Grenada in the Caribbean Sea during Operation Nickle Grass.

*Worm's-eye view of an F-117A shows landing gear and air data probe details.*

The invasion was swift and the action was over almost before it had started. Therefore, the combat debut of the F-117A stealth fighter was put off; its veil of secrecy remained intact. But some 30 months later, its veil nearly lifted for Operation El Dorado Canyon.

On 14 April 1986, during Operation El Dorado Canyon, the United States bombed Libya in retaliation for its state-sponsored terrorism. By this time the Nighthawks had some 30 F-117A aircraft ready for combat, and the service of the still-Top Secret stealth fighter was seriously considered. But once more, the action was short-lived and the prowess of the Black Jet was not shown.

Just 44 months later, however, the newly formed 37th TFW with its almost complete fleet of F-117As rolled onto the "highway to the danger zone" to participate in Operation Just Cause.

## Operation Just Cause

On 19 December 1989, just 13 months after the Pentagon had disclosed the existence of the F-117A, the world's first stealth fighter made its combat debut. Yet, at the time, very little was known about the Black Jet.

At the beginning of Operation Just Cause, six F-117As flew nonstop to Panama via aerial refueling from Tonopah—without detection. Then, to stun and disorient Panama Defense Force (PDF) troops, two lead F-117As each dropped one conventional 2,000-

pound device at Rio Hato; these are thought to have been laser-guided GBU-10 Paveway II 2,000-pound bombs. The combat debut of the F-117A stealth fighter was reported to be a complete success, but this was not the case.

As announced later, one of the 2,000-pound devices hit off target. Worse, the USAF did not disclose the bombing error to the Pentagon until a Pentagon F-117A media event had concluded on 3 April 1990. This event, of course, left Defense Secretary Richard B. (Dick) Cheney touting the aircraft's bombing accuracy for some three months after the bombing mistake in Panama.

Moreover, Pentagon spokesman Pete Williams, who had briefed the media on the F-117A stealth fighter on the morning of 3 April, was not made aware of the bombing error until the afternoon of 3 April. Subsequently, Williams had to confirm that one of the F-117As had dropped a 2,000-pound bomb some distance away from its intended target. He explained: "The pilots were told to drop their bombs no closer than 50 meters" from two separate PDF barracks buildings, "But due to a last minute misunderstanding between the two pilots, the second F-117 dropped its bomb on a hillside some distance away. The first bomb hit 55 meters from one of the barracks buildings, but the second bomb was way off target."

Williams also acknowledged that despite weeks of special preparation for his F-117A press conference, during which he disclosed long-secret details, "I didn't know" about the bombing error. "It was news to us [the Pentagon]," he added. Asked when the USAF told the Pentagon, Williams answered that the Pentagon was not informed about the bombing error until the afternoon of 3 April, hours after the morning F-117A media briefing had concluded. The entire episode was not made public until 6 April 1990.

According to one expert who wishes to remain anonymous, Operation Just Cause gave the public a bad impression about the usefulness of the F-117A. Many factors contributed to the bombing error in Panama including weather, last-minute mission planning changes, pilot error, etc. As a test case, it was a poor and misleading example of what the Black Jet is capable of doing.

Operations Desert Shield and Desert Storm certainly attest to the F-117A's potential and give credence to what our anonymous expert had to say about the F-117A's combat debut some 10 months before the beginning of Operation Desert Shield.

## Operation Desert Shield

In response to the aggression of Iraq into Kuwait, and to deter such action into other Middle Eastern countries, the 37th TFW deployed its 415th TFS to Saudi Arabia in support of Operation Desert Shield on 19 August 1990. As tensions built within the region, a second squadron, the 416th TFS, was also deployed in December 1990. Subsequently, in January 1991, a portion of the wing's 417th TFTS also deployed. This gave the U.S. Central Command the precision firepower of state-of-the-art F-117A stealth fighters.

Then, in the early morning of 17 January 1991, the 37th TFW's mission changed when U.S.-led coalition forces initiated their air campaign to expel the Iraqi military forces from Kuwait as Operation Desert Storm began.

## Operation Desert Storm

To initiate Operation Desert Storm, an F-117A Black Jet delivered the first bomb on a military target in central Baghdad, Iraq, just prior to 3 A.M. local time; mission planners had targeted F-117A aircraft against critical strategic Iraqi command and control installations. Other vital targets assigned to the 37th TFW included key communications centers; research, development, production, and storage facilities for nuclear and chemical weapons; and a variety of other important targets, especially hardened aircraft shelters on numerous Iraqi airfields.

In preparation for what became a 100-hour ground war (no one knew just how long it would last), theater planners also tasked Black Jet pilots against critical Iraqi resupply lines which included key bridges, railroad switching yards, and major highways. In fact, just before the ground war began, F-117As successfully destroyed a complex of pumping stations and distribution networks designed to feed oil into anti-personnel fire trenches along the southern borders of Kuwait and Iraq.

In the opening shot of the air campaign against Iraq, an F-117A dropped a laser-guided 2,000-pound GBU-27 Paveway III bomb through the roof of the general communications building in downtown Baghdad and into the heart of its communications center. In another attack on the communications building next to the Tigris River, another GBU-27 Paveway III was shown to precisely enter an air shaft in the center of the roof atop the multistory building before blowing all four of its walls out.

Colonel Al Whitley, who took command of the 37th TFW just before its deployment to Saudi Arabia, told his pilots what to expect: "It would seem a little bit like fear, perhaps a little bit like anxiety. But not to worry, because we are well-equipped."

Tony Landis

*F-117A at Nellis AFB.*

*Eight F-117As on Nellis AFB hot line after returning home from Saudi Arabia.*

*37th TFW commander's F-117A,* The Toxic Avenger, *shows the personal equipment pod mounted on the left-hand bomb rack.*

A large contingent of allied air forces aircraft blitzed Iraqi forces and high-value targets as Operation Desert Storm began the offensive to liberate Kuwait from the occupation forces of Iraq. And, of course, the F-117A stealth fighter was a major contributor in what may be recorded as the most intense aerial offensive in history. For six weeks, allied air forces hammered Iraqi military targets to pave the way for the eventual withdrawal of Iraqi forces from the tiny emirate.

Hundreds of coalition forces aircraft—specifically, those of the United States, Great Britain, France, Kuwait, and Saudi Arabia—conducted an intense aerial bombardment to destroy Iraq's nuclear, biological, and chemical warfare facilities; its air force; naval force; antiaircraft artillery and missile batteries; radar installations; ballistic missile launchers; command and control network; resupply routes; and Iraqi troop concentrations. For the most part, these were left waste.

During the first three weeks of aerial activity, during which more than 42,000 combat missions (sorties) were flown, F-117A Black Jets obliterated many hardened targets with unprecedented precision. The number of combat sorties flown by allied aircraft grew to an average rate of 3,000 per 24-hour period. In all, more than 110,000 combat sorties were flown by all types of aircraft. While some types of aircraft were lost for various reasons, not one F-117 was hit, shot down, or lost due to mechanical failure. U.S. aircraft alone off-loaded 84,500 tons of ordnance on Iraq and occupied Kuwait. Of that total amount, precision-guided bombs accounted for some 9 percent, or 7,400 tons. During the Persian Gulf War, then, stealth proved its worth on a daily basis and the tactical surprise was due in part to the difficulties any defense has in 'seeing' low-observable aircraft. The F-117A's concealment, deception, and evasiveness proved its survivability, and its laser-guided bombs fell with extreme accuracy.

As one result of Operation Desert Storm, there is little doubt that future military strike aircraft—whether attack, bomber, or fighter designation—will employ some measure of low-observable technology for survivability. USAF officials are lauding—and rightly so—the performance of the F-117A, claiming that it has established the ascendancy of stealth technologies. In the Black Jet, a bona fide star has emerged.

The Lockheed F-117A was a workhorse during the Persian Gulf War, the epitomy of a stealth fighter/attack aircraft. In the six-week-long air campaign, the 37th TFW flew 1,271 combat sorties, logged more than 6,900 combat hours, and maintained an 85.5 percent mission-capable rate, which is equal to other high-technology aircraft. The 43 F-117s deployed to Saudi Arabia delivered more than 2,000 tons of ordnance in a precise manner. And, although the F-117s represented less than 3 percent of the armada deployed by the USAF, they attacked some 40 percent of the high-value targets that are struck by the coalition forces. The average combat sortie time for the F-117A was 5.4 hours. Each airplane averaged 29.7 combat sorties, while operating with impunity.

Most of the F-117s that were deployed to Saudi Arabia have returned home. A major homecoming event occurred at Nellis AFB on 1 April 1991. Some F-117s still remain in Saudi Arabia for obvious reasons, while others are on temporary duty at places such as Langley AFB, Virginia, and other close-to-the-Middle-East bases in case a rapid deployment is required of them.

The verdict on covert tactics is in: They work.

# 5

# Stealth Aircraft
# Past, Present, and Future

LOCKHEED—its Skunk Works in particular—is the undisputed leader in the development of stealth aircraft—past, present and future. Only now are other airframe contractors beginning to share the stealth spotlight with the Lockheed Skunk Works. Lockheed's head start on low-observable technology has generated a number of notable and successful aircraft, including the U-2, A-12/YF-12/SR-71 series, TR-1, and the F-22, which recently won the USAF Advanced Tactical Fighter (ATF) competition.

## Lockheed's Stealthy Forerunners

Derived from a top secret Central Intelligence Agency (CIA), Department of Defense, and U.S. Air Force program code named Bald Eagle, Lockheed created a subsonic high-altitude spyplane that was designated U-2 (Utility-2) to hide its true mission, tactical reconnaissance. Flown by Lockheed's famed chief engineering test pilot Anthony W. (Tony) LeVier, the number one U-2 made its official first flight on 8 August 1955 from an obscure test range in Nellis AFB, Nevada.

Having been specifically created to covertly overfly the Union of Soviet Socialist Republics (USSR) in the CIA's attempt to keep a watchful eye on this Cold War competitor, the presence of the U-2 was discovered much sooner than expected, and the USSR did something about it. On 1 May 1960, the U-2B being flown by Francis Gary Powers was discovered and shot down with an improved surface-to-air missile (SAM). One reason the USSR was successful in shooting down Powers' U-2B was that this type of reconnaissance aircraft was not survivable enough to prevent radar acquisition and lock-on, nor fast enough with its subsonic speed to escape the multisonic SAM. After the Powers incident,

Lockheed

*The number one Lockheed U-2.*

Lockheed

*An early Lockheed A-12.*

spyplane activities, especially over the USSR, were immediately discontinued. A newer and more survivable type of aircraft was needed.

Even before the highly publicized U-2 incident occurred, the CIA, DOD, and USAF recognized the need for an improved manned aircraft that would be capable of effective photographic reconnaissance with little or no danger to the aircraft and its crew. Thus, under the top secret Oxcart program, a new Lockheed design designated A-12 (formerly A-11) was approved in 1959 as the U-2 follow-on. As the result, Lockheed was authorized to produce twelve A-12 aircraft. The number one A-12 was officially flight-tested by

Lockheed test pilot Lou Schalk on 30 April 1962 somewhere within the Nellis AFB test range complex.

The differences between the U-2 of 1955 and the A-12 of 1962 are vast. Basically, the latter was optimized to defeat the USSR's improved radar network and SAMs with its much higher triplesonic speed (i.e., if detected, it would be out of range by the time a SAM arrived at the point of discovery; thus, its interception was next to impossible).

An A-12 spinoff was the Lockheed YF-12 Improved Manned Interceptor (IMI) aircraft, created to supplement and replace the Convair F-106 Delta Dart. First flown at Nellis by Lockheed test pilot James D. (Jim) Eastham on 7 August 1963, the YF-12 was a spectacular performer. However, procurement funds for the IMI were never fully approved and the promising IMI program was cancelled after only three YF-12s had been built.

*The number one Lockheed YF-12.*

Although the A-12 was much harder to shoot down than the U-2 because of its triplesonic speed and improved electronic countermeasures (ECM), there was room for further advances in the brand-new field of low-observable technology aircraft. Therefore, the Lockheed Skunk Works continued to further reduce aircraft signatures—infrared, radar cross section, and so on. An early result was the Lockheed SR-71, successor to the A-12, that was first flown on 22 December 1964 by Lockheed test pilot Robert J. (Bob) Gilliland.

The Lockheed SR-71 served faithfully with the USAF for a quarter of a century before its recent out-in-style retirement from the Strategic Air Command (SAC). On the day of its retirement, the SR-71 destined for eternal display at the National Air and Space

*Lockheed SR-71 Blackbird.*

Museum in Washington, D.C., flew coast-to-coast across the contiguous United States in a mere 68 minutes!

During the SR-71's heyday, many versions of the U-2 spyplane, including the much-improved U-2R, remained active in a number of roles (most of which are classified). The U-2's ultimate successor, the Lockheed TR-1, is more advanced and more survivable than its U-2 series predecessors.

*Lockheed TR-1 Reconnaissance Star.*

The Lockheed F-22 of today—and tomorrow—is the world's first air superiority fighter with dedicated low-observable technology characteristics. It was designed from the outset to hide signatures and for matchless performance in air-to-air combat. If the F-22 Advanced Tactical Fighter (ATF) goes into production, it will rewrite the book on fighter aircraft, for it embodies all that has been learned about fighter aircraft since the advent of the Curtiss P-1 Hawk of 1925.

Lockheed

*Lockheed YF-22A Advanced Tactical Fighter.*

In reviewing their accomplishments in the world of stealth aircraft, then, it becomes clear that Lockheed is the current leader in the creation of such air vehicles. Moreover, it becomes obvious why Lockheed was the single-source airframe contractor on the F-117 program. At the time, Lockheed simply had no peers.

*Rockwell B-1B Lancer.*

## Stealth Today

It is another story today. The application of low-observable technology on military aircraft is becoming quite common. In various ways, using different approaches, reduced signatures have been achieved on strategic bomber aircraft such as the Rockwell B-1 Lancer and the Northrop B-2 stealth bomber. The latter, incidentally, relies on curved and angled exterior surfaces to reduce its RCS rather than angles alone as on the F-117A Black Jet—two very different trains of thought, by different manufacturers, to achieve the very same goal.

The AX (Attack, Experimental), a proposed carrier-based stealth attack airplane being designed to fill the void that was created with the recent cancellation of the A-12 Avenger II, will use low-observable technology to bolster its own survivability. So will helicopters such as the proposed LH (Light Helicopter) of the Boeing and Sikorsky team. Indeed, stealth aircraft are here to stay.

*The number one Northrop B-2.*

Northrop

To create new and improved stealth aircraft for today and tomorrow, there are some established rules to follow. These rules, in part, are as follows:

- Pay close attention to aircraft shaping, as this alone can reduce an aircraft's radar cross section by as much as 85 percent.
- Use accurate models to measure radar returns before the aircraft is built: be persistent.
- Mask power emissions from the aircraft's avionics.
- Employ non-augmented (non-afterburning) turbofan engines to generate less heat and lower infrared signature; mask engine air inlets and exhaust outlets to reduce the radar cross section and infrared signature of the powerplant(s).
- Construct airframes (inside and outside) with composite materials which are lighter, stronger, and more radar-absorbing than metallic alloys; use radar-absorbing materials on the exterior of the aircraft to mask rivets, skin separations, etc.
- Employ blended and/or retractable external antennas, air data probes, and inflight refueling receptacles on the aircraft.

There are, of course, many other parameters to address before a stealth aircraft can be successful, but these are classified. The Lockheed F-117A Black Jet is considered to be a "first generation" stealth aircraft. If the B-2 is a "second generation" stealth aircraft, what would a "third generation" stealth aircraft entail?

## Tomorrow's Rumors

There are persistent rumors of other flying stealth-type aircraft that have not been confirmed by the Pentagon. One rumor has a large delta-shaped aircraft flying around. Another tells of a flying air vehicle shaped like a pumpkin seed. But the strongest rumor thus far concerns a triangular-shaped tactical reconnaissance stealth aircraft designated TR-3, named Black Manta, and possibly produced by Northrop.

The Northrop TR-3 Black Manta, if it exists, is said to be a spinoff of the Tactical High Altitude Penetrator (THAP) program of 1976; in 1981, a THAP demonstrator was flown. The rumor mill has it that as many as 30 TR-3s could be in operation to support stealth strike aircraft.

However, without proof of such aircraft, these persistent rumors remain unsubstantiated and vague.

## Conclusions

Since the mid 1970s, when serious activity to dramatically reduce aircraft radar cross-section signature began under the DARPA/USAF Have Blue XST project, low-observable technology for manned aircraft—specifically the F-117A—has been validated during Operation Desert Storm.

This remarkable program had a dominant influence on consolidating the development time for the "first generation" low-observable technologies employed. In addition to the aircraft design and materials development activity required, even the means of supporting radar cross-section models had to be invented to permit verification of predicted signatures under Project Harvey. The XST program did more than introduce stealth design approaches and criteria. The operational analyses clearly indicated an overwhelming impact of stealth on mission effectiveness, even when aircraft propulsion system effi-

*A family portrait of Lockheed Blackbirds—the F-117A, the U-2, and the SR-71.*

ciency was compromised (i.e., low-thrust and non-augmented engines). It was demonstrated that the detectability reductions shown during this program not only increased survivability but had a dramatic influence on restored operating freedom and lethality to the user for a variety of tasks.

The achievement of low-observability impacts almost every aspect of aircraft design. The radar cross section of a manned air vehicle is the collection of the individual returns from a large collection of radar scatterers. Although internal gear in an aircraft appears to be an exception to this rule, the basic approach used for the XST and subsequent designs is to focus edge returns by the use of straight—not rounded—line planforms. Finally, all returns are reduced by the prudent use of radar-absorbing materials.

The Lockheed F-117A is currently out of production, but, still in demand. At this writing, the 37th TFW has 56 operational F-117A aircraft, or enough for three 18-plane squadrons. And, at this writing, the Senate Armed Services Committee wanted to fund at least 24 "new" production F-117As and reopen the production line that closed down in July 1990. On 1 November 1991, it was announced that 12, not 24, new F-117As might be funded and produced.

Apparently, the history of the world's first operational low-observable fighter is far from over.

# Appendix

# F-117A Facts and Figures

## Have Blue Specifications

| | |
|---|---|
| **Type** | Single-seat, twin-engine Experimental Survivable Testbed (XST) |
| **User** | USAF/DARPA |
| **Length** | 38 feet, 0 inches |
| **Height** | 7 feet, 6 inches |
| **Wingspan** | 22 feet, 0 inches |
| **Gross weight** | 12,000 pounds |
| $V_{max}$ | 0.80 Mach |
| **Endurance** | 1 hour |
| **Armament** | None |
| **Propulsion** | Two non-augmented General Electric J85 turbojet engines |

## F-117A Specifications

| | |
|---|---|
| **Type** | Single-seat, twin-engine fighter/attack airplane |
| **User** | USAF/TAC |
| **Length** | 65 feet, 11 inches |
| **Height** | 12 feet, 5 inches |
| **Wingspan** | 43 feet, 4 inches |
| **Empty weight** | 28,500 pounds |
| **Gross weight** | 52,500 pounds |
| **Fuel weight** | 19,000 pounds |
| **Combat radius** | 900 mi. (unrefueled) |
| $V_{max}$ | 0.80 Mach |
| **Armament** | Laser-guided conventional bombs; tactical munitions dispensers; nuclear bombs |
| **Propulsion** | Two non-augmented 10,000-pound thrust class General Electric F404-GE-F1D2 turbofan engines |

## Have Blue Production

| Airframe | Serial Number | Comment |
|---|---|---|
| Have Blue-1 | 1001 | First flown 12/77; crashed 5/78 (total loss) |
| Have Blue-2 | 1002 | First flown 6/78; crashed 7/79 (total loss) |

## Senior Trend F-117A Full-Scale Development Production

| Airframe | Serial Number | Comment |
|---|---|---|
| F-117A (FSD-1) | 79-01780 | First flown 6/81; disposition unknown |
| F-117A (FSD-2) | 79-01781 | To Air Force Museum on 7/17/91 |
| F-117A (FSD-3) | 79-01782 | Disposition unknown |
| F-117A (FSD-4) | 79-01783 | Disposition unknown |
| F-117A (FSD-5) | 79-01784 | Disposition unknown |

Note: Service test Y prefix was added to the F-117A FSD aircraft at the Air Force Museum; thus current designation is YF-117A. Two F-117A FSD aircraft are still flying; two are in storage.

## Senior Trend F-117A Production

| Airframe | Serial Number | Comment |
|---|---|---|
| F-117A | 80-01785 | First flight attempted on 4/20/82; crashed (crashed prior to USAF/TAC acceptance; thus not counted in production total). |
| F-117A-1 | 80-01786 | |
| F-117A-2 | 80-01787 | |
| F-117A-3 | 80-01788 | |
| F-117A-4 | 80-01789 | |
| F-117A-5 | 80-01790 | |
| F-117A-6 | 80-01791 | |
| F-117A-7 | 81-01792 | Crashed on 7/11/86; Maj. Ross Mulhare killed (aircraft total loss). |
| F-117A-8 | 81-01793 | |
| F-117A-9 | 81-01794 | |
| F-117A-10 | 81-01795 | |
| F-117A-11 | 81-01796 | |
| F-117A-12 | 81-01797 | |
| F-117A-13 | 81-01798 | |
| F-117A-14 | 82-01799 | With delivery of this airframe on 10/28/83, the 4450th TG (now 37th TFW) achieved IOC. |
| F-117A-15 | 82-01800 | |
| F-117A-16 | 82-01801 | |
| F-117A-17 | 82-01802 | |
| F-117A-18 | 82-01803 | |
| F-117A-19 | 82-01804 | |
| F-117A-20 | 82-01805 | |
| F-117A-21 | 82-01806 | |
| F-117A-22 | 82-01807 | |
| F-117A-23 | 83-01808 | Only F-117A with Fiscal Year 1983 prefix. |
| F-117A-24 | 84-01809 | |
| F-117A-25 | 84-01810 | |
| F-117A-26 | 84-01811 | |
| F-117A-27 | 84-01812 | |
| F-117A-28 | 85-01813 | Wing commander's airplane. |
| F-117A-29 | 85-01814 | |
| F-117A-30 | 85-01815 | Crashed on 10/14/87; Maj. Michael Stewart killed (aircraft total loss). |
| F-117A-31 | 85-01816 | |
| F-117A-32 | 85-01817 | |
| F-117A-33 | 85-01818 | |
| F-117A-34 | 85-01819 | |
| F-117A-35 | 85-01820 | |
| F-117A-36 | 85-01821 | |
| F-117A-37 | 85-01822 | |

| Airframe | Serial Number | Comment |
|----------|---------------|---------|
| F-117A-38 | 85-01823 | |
| F-117A-39 | 85-01824 | |
| F-117A-40 | 84-01825 | |
| F-117A-41 | 84-01826 | |
| F-117A-42 | 84-01827 | |
| F-117A-43 | 84-01828 | |
| F-117A-44 | 85-01829 | |
| F-117A-45 | 85-01830 | |
| F-117A-46 | 85-01831 | |
| F-117A-47 | 85-01832 | |
| F-117A-48 | 85-01833 | |
| F-117A-49 | 85-01834 | |
| F-117A-50 | 85-01835 | |
| F-117A-51 | 85-01836 | |
| F-117A-52 | 86-01837 | |
| F-117A-53 | 86-01838 | |
| F-117A-54 | 86-01839 | |
| F-117A-55 | 86-01840 | |
| F-117A-56 | 87-01841 | |
| F-117A-57 | 87-01842 | |
| F-117A-58 | 87-01843 | |
| F-117A-59 | 87-01844 | Delivered to USAF/TAC on 7/12/90; last F-117A produced |

## F-117A Major Subcontractors and Suppliers

The F-117A program is supported by major subcontractors and suppliers. Those whose participation has been declassified are as follows:

**Allied Signal Aerospace Company,** Torrance, California.

- Auxiliary Power System
- Emergency Power System
- Environment Control System
- Air Data Transducer

**American Fuel Cells Coated Fabric Company,** Magnolia, Arizona.

- Fuel cells

**Astech/MCI Manufacturing, Incorporated,** Santa Ana, California.

- Engine exhaust tailpipes

**Delco Electronics,** Goleta, California.

- Digital Tape Set 1553 Computer
- Laboratory support equipment

**Explosive Technology,** Fairfield, California.

- Formable explosive charges for tailhook cover

**F.L. Aerospace, Grimes Division,** Urbana, Ohio.

- Secondary cockpit lighting
- Inflight refueling lights
- Electro-luminescent panels

**General Electric Company,** Binghamton, New York.

- Engines
- Fuel quantity system
- Engine performance indicator
- Engine signal detector unit
- Generator

**Goodyear Tire & Rubber Company,** Akron, Ohio.

- Tires

**GTT Industries, Incorporated,** Westlake Village, California.

- Hardware/software for PC-based Automated Test System

**Harris Corporation,** Melbourne, Florida.

- Digital moving map radar
- Digital tactical/display system

**HITCO,** Gardena, California.

- Item(s) unknown

**Honeywell, Incorporated,** St. Petersburg, Florida.

- Radar altimeter
- Inertial Navigation System
- Air data computer
- Color multipurpose display system

**International Business Machines,** Oswego, New York.

- Mission computer

**Kaiser Electronics,** San Jose, California.

- Projection Interface Unit (PIU)
- Projection Display Unit (PDU)

**Lear Astronics Corporation,** Santa Monica, California.

- Flight Control Computer/Navigation Interface/Autopilot Computer (NIAC) system

**Link Flight Simulator Corporation,** Binghamton, New York.

- Weapon system trainers
- Software for simulator

**Lockheed Aircraft Services Company,** Ontario, California.

- Mobile Training Unit

**Loral Aircraft Braking System,** Akron, Ohio.

- Brakes
- Wheels
- Anti-skid brake control system

**Lucas Aerospace Power Transmission Corporation,** Utica, New York.

- Power transmission shaft

**Menasco,** Burbank, California.

- Main landing gear
- Nose landing gear

**National Waterlift Division of Pneumo Corporation,** Kalamazoo, Michigan.

- Servo actuators

**Northrop,** Norwood, Maine.

- Rate gyro

**Parker-Hannifin Corporation,** Irvine, California.

- Fuel system values

**Pioneer Aerospace Corporation,** South Windsor, Connecticut.

- Parachute system

**Sargent Controls,** Yorba Linda, California.

- Control quadrant (throttle)
- Switch matrix

**SCI Technology, Incorporated,** Huntsville, Alabama.

- Data bus coupler

**Sierracin/Sylmar Corporation,** Sylmar, California.

- Windshield panels

**SLI Avionic Systems Corporation,** Grand Rapids, Michigan.

- Expanded Data Transfer System
- Altitude Heading Reference System

**Sundstrand Corporation,** Rockford, Illinois.

- Air turbine starter

**Teledyne Controls,** West Los Angeles, California.

- Annunciator panel

**Western Gear Corporation,** City of Industry, California.

- Aircraft Mounted Accessory Drive (AMAD) Gearbox

**XAR Industries,** City of Industry, California.

- Inflight refueling valve

There are, of course, many other subcontractors and suppliers on the F-117A program. It is not known when their respective contributions will be declassified.

## 4450th Tactical Group (TG) and 37th Tactical Fighter Wing (TFW) Commanders

| Commander | Tenure (approximate) | Group/Wing |
|---|---|---|
| Col. Robert J. Jackson | 10/79 to 5/82 | 4450th TG |
| Col. James S. Allen | 5/82 to 6/84 | 4450th TG |
| Col. Howell M. Estes III | 6/84 to 12/86 | 4450th TG |
| Col. Michael J. Harris | 12/86 to ? | 4450th TG |
| Col. Michael C. Short | ? to 8/88 | 4450th TG |
| Col. Anthony J. Tolin | 8/88 to 8/90 | 4450th TG/37th TFW* |
| Col. Alton C. Whitley | 8/90 to? | 37th TFW |

*The 4450th TG became the 37th TFW in October 1989, some fourteen months after Col. Tolin became commander of the 4450th TG.

## Known Operation Desert Storm F-117A Weapons Bay Artwork

| Tail Number | Name |
|---|---|
| 786 | War Pig |
| 791 | Lazy Ace |
| 793 | Tritonal Express |
| 794 | Delta Dawn |
| 796 | Fatal Attraction |
| 798 | Aces and Eights |
| 801 | Perpetrator |
| 806 | Something Wicked |
| 807 | Chicken Hawk |
| 808 | Thor |
| 810 | Dark Angel |
| 811 | Double Down |
| 813 | The Toxic Avenger |
| 814 | Final Verdict |

| Tail Number | Name |
| --- | --- |
| 816 | Lone Wolf |
| 821 | Nachtfalke |
| 825 | Mad Max |
| 830 | Black Assassin |
| 835 | The Dragon |
| 836 | Christine |
| 837 | Habu II |
| 838 | Magic Hammer |
| 839 | Midnight Reaper |
| 841 | Mystic Warrior |
| 843 | Affectionately Christine |

Note: This is the only available list of F-117A weapons bay artwork (and aircraft names) at this writing. Compiled by MSgt. Bobby Shelton, 37th TFW Public Affairs.

# Bibliography

*Air Force* magazine, published monthly by the Air Force Association, Arlington, Virginia; various issues from January 1989.

*Aviation Week and Space Technology* magazine, published weekly by McGraw-Hill, New York, New York; various issues since November 1988.

Dane, Abe. "Black Jet." *Popular Mechanics* magazine, New York, New York, July 1990.

Goodall, James. *F-117 Stealth in Action.* Squadron/Signal Publications, Inc., Carrollton, Texas, 1991.

*Jane's All the World's Aircraft.* McGraw-Hill, New York, New York, 1990-91.

Kennedy, Bob. "Night Striker." *Airpower* magazine, Granada Hills, California, September 1990.

Miller, Jay. *Lockheed F-117 Stealth Fighter.* Aerofax, Inc., Arlington, Texas, 1990.

O'Leary, Michael. "Last F-117A Delivered." *Air Combat* magazine, Canoga Park, California, October 1990.

Sweetman, Bill and Goodall, James. *Lockheed F-117A.* Motorbooks International, Osceola, Wisconsin, 1990.

# Index